Monet's IMPRESSIONS

Words and pictures by
Claude Monet

THE METROPOLITAN MUSEUM OF ART
New York

chronicle books · san francisco

Landscape is only an impression,
its appearance changing at every moment.

~Claude Monet

In trying to capture how a landscape looked in a particular light at a particular moment, French artist Claude Monet closely studied nature and worked directly on the spot, sometimes turning from one canvas to the next as the light changed. He and other artists in his circle came to be known as the Impressionists, a name taken from the title of Monet's painting *Impression, Sunrise* (above).

Monet wrote letters to his family and friends, and often spoke about his work. Here are some of his paintings paired with his words.

I paint like a bird sings,

in every harmony.

Fresh, foggy mornings,

light spilling everywhere,

sudden bursts of sun,

the beauty of the air.

Flowers in the spring,

trees against the blue sea,

huge waves, splendidly wild,

snow, a white immensity.

Water and reflections,

water, water lilies,

a passing cloud,

a freshening breeze.

The sun, an enormous fireball,

setting gloriously.

The works of art reproduced in this book are by Claude Monet (French, 1840–1926). The words in the text were taken from Monet's letters to family and friends and from articles in which he was quoted. In some cases, the words were translated verbatim; in others, a free translation was used. The credits below list the sources of the quotes. The numbered letters can be found in Daniel Wildenstein's *Claude Monet : biographie et catalogue raisonné*, 1974–85. —L. F.

Gustave Geffroy, "Histoire de l'Impressionnisme," *La Vie Artistique*, 1894

The Magpie
Oil on canvas, 35 x 51⅕ in., 1868–69
Musée d'Orsay, Paris
Photograph: Erich Lessing / Art Resource, New York

Letter to Alice Monet, March 18, 1900 (no. 1582)

Camille Monet (1847–1879) in the Garden at Argenteuil
Oil on canvas, 32⅛ x 23⅝ in., 1876
The Metropolitan Museum of Art, New York
The Walter H. and Leonore Annenberg Collection,
Gift of Walter H. and Leonore Annenberg, 2000,
Bequest of Walter H. Annenberg, 2002   2000.93.1

François Thiébault-Sisson, "Autour de Claude Monet, Anecdotes et souvenirs," *Le Temps*, January 8, 1927

Morning on the Seine near Giverny
Oil on canvas, 32⅛ x 36⅝ in., 1897
The Metropolitan Museum of Art, New York
Bequest of Julia W. Emmons, 1956   56.135.4

Gustave Geffroy, *Claude Monet : sa vie, son temps, son oeuvre*, 1922

Landscape at Zaandam
Oil on canvas, 18 x 26⅜ in., 1871–72
The Metropolitan Museum of Art, New York
Robert Lehman Collection, 1975   1975.1.196

François Thiébault-Sisson, "Autour de Claude Monet, Anecdotes et souvenirs," *Le Temps*, January 8, 1927

The Parc Monceau
Oil on canvas, 28⅝ x 21⅜ in., 1878
THE METROPOLITAN MUSEUM OF ART, New York
The Mr. and Mrs. Henry Ittleson Jr. Purchase
Fund, 1959   59.142

Hermann Bang, *Journal*, April 6, 1895

Garden at Sainte-Adresse
Oil on canvas, 38⅝ x 51⅛ in., 1867
THE METROPOLITAN MUSEUM OF ART, New York
Purchase, special contributions and funds given or
bequeathed by friends of the Museum, 1967   67.241

François Thiébault-Sisson, "Les Nymphéas de Claude Monet,"
La Revue de l'art ancien et moderne, June–December 1927

Camille Monet and a Child in the Artist's Garden in Argenteuil
Oil on canvas, 21¾ x 25½ in., 1875
MUSEUM OF FINE ARTS, Boston
Anonymous gift in memory of Mr. and
Mrs. Edwin S. Webster, 1976   1976.833
Photograph © 2009 Museum of Fine Arts, Boston

Letter to Alice Hoschedé, January 26, 1884 (no. 394)

Bordighera
Oil on canvas, 25½ x 32 in., 1884
THE ART INSTITUTE OF CHICAGO
Potter Palmer Collection   1922.426
Photography © The Art Institute of Chicago

Letters to Alice Hoschedé, November 27, 1885 (no. 631), and G. Caillebotte, October 11, 1886 (no. 709)

The Manneporte (Étretat)
Oil on canvas, 25⅜ x 32 in., 1883
THE METROPOLITAN MUSEUM OF ART, New York
Bequest of William Church Osborn, 1951   51.30.5

Letter to Blanche Hoschedé, March 1, 1895 (no. 1276)

Ice Floes
Oil on canvas, 26 x 39½ in., 1898
THE METROPOLITAN MUSEUM OF ART, New York
H. O. Havemeyer Collection, Bequest of
Mrs. H. O. Havemeyer, 1929   29.100.108

Gustave Geffroy, *Claude Monet : sa vie, son temps, son oeuvre*, 1922

La Grenouillère
Oil on canvas, 29⅜ x 39¼ in., 1869
THE METROPOLITAN MUSEUM OF ART, New York
H. O. Havemeyer Collection, Bequest of
Mrs. H. O. Havemeyer, 1929   29.100.112

Letter to Raymond Koechlin, January 15, 1915
(no. 2142)

Water Lilies
Oil on canvas, 39¾ x 78¾ in., 1919
THE METROPOLITAN MUSEUM OF ART, New York
The Walter H. and Leonore Annenberg Collection,
Gift of Walter H. and Leonore Annenberg, 1998,
Bequest of Walter H. Annenberg, 2002   1998.325.2

François Thiébault-Sisson, "Les Nymphéas de Claude Monet," *La Revue de l'art ancien et moderne*, June–December 1927

Poppy Fields Near Argenteuil
Oil on canvas, 21¼ x 29 in., 1875
THE METROPOLITAN MUSEUM OF ART, New York
The Walter H. and Leonore Annenberg Collection,
Gift of Walter H. and Leonore Annenberg, 2001,
Bequest of Walter H. Annenberg, 2002   2001.202.5

François Thiébault-Sisson, "Les Nymphéas de Claude Monet," *La Revue de l'art ancien et moderne*, June–December 1927

Woman with a Parasol—Madame Monet and Her Son
Oil on canvas, 39⅝ x 31⅞ in., 1875
NATIONAL GALLERY OF ART, Washington, D.C.
Collection of Mr. and Mrs. Paul Mellon   1983.1.29
Image courtesy of the Board of Trustees,
National Gallery of Art

Letter to Alice Monet, March 9, 1900 (no. 1527)

Setting Sun on the Seine at Lavacourt, Winter Effect
Oil on canvas, 39¾ x 59 in., 1880
MUSÉE DU PETIT PALAIS, Paris
Photograph: Réunion des Musées Nationaux / Art
Resource, New York

Letter to Alice Monet, February 14, 1900 (no. 1507)

San Giorgio Maggiore by Twilight
Oil on canvas, 25⅝ x 36⅝ in., 1908
NATIONAL MUSEUM OF WALES, Cardiff
The Davies Sisters Collection; Bequest, Gwendoline
Davies, 1952   NMW A 2485
© National Museum of Wales

FRONT COVER:
Bridge over a Pond of Water Lilies (detail). Claude Monet, French, 1840-1926.
Oil on canvas, 36½ x 29 in., 1899. THE METROPOLITAN MUSEUM OF ART, New York.
H. O. Havemeyer Collection, Bequest of Mrs. H. O. Havemeyer, 1929   29.100.113

BACK COVER:
Poppy Fields Near Argenteuil. Claude Monet, French, 1840-1926.
Oil on canvas, 21¼ x 29 in., 1875. THE METROPOLITAN MUSEUM OF ART, New York.
The Walter H. and Leonore Annenberg Collection, Gift of Walter H. and Leonore Annenberg, 2001,
Bequest of Walter H. Annenberg, 2002   2001.202.5

TITLE PAGE:
Jean Monet (1867-1913) on His Hobby Horse. Claude Monet, French, 1840-1926.
Oil on canvas, 23⅞ x 29¼ in., 1872. THE METROPOLITAN MUSEUM OF ART, New York.
Gift of Sara Lee Corporation, 2000   2000.195

PAGE 6:
Self-Portrait with a Beret. Claude Monet, French, 1840-1926.
Oil on canvas, 22 x 18⅛ in., 1886. PRIVATE COLLECTION.
Photograph © Lefevre Fine Art Ltd., London / The Bridgeman Art Library International

PAGE 7:
Maurice Guillemot, "Claude Monet," *La Revue illustrée,* March 15, 1898,
and W. G. C. Byvanck, *Un Hollandais à Paris en 1891,* 1892

Impression, Sunrise. Claude Monet, French, 1840-1926. Oil on canvas, 18⅞ x 24¾ in., 1872.
MUSÉE MARMOTTAN, Paris.
Photograph: Erich Lessing / Art Resource, New York

Published by The Metropolitan Museum of Art and Chronicle Books LLC.

Produced by the Department of Special Publications, The Metropolitan Museum of Art:
Robie Rogge, Publishing Manager; Linda Falken, Senior Editor; Atif Toor, Designer; Mary Wong, Assistant Production Manager.

Photography by The Metropolitan Museum of Art Photograph Studio.

Manufactured in China.

Library of Congress Cataloging-in-Publication Data

Monet, Claude, 1840-1926.
   Monet's impressions : words and pictures / by Claude Monet.
      p. cm.
   ISBN 978-1-58839-306-7 (The Metropolitan Museum of Art) —
   ISBN 978-0-8118-7056-6 (Chronicle Books)
   1. Monet, Claude, 1840-1926—Themes, motives. 2. Monet, Claude,
1840-1926—Quotations. I. Title.
   ND553.M7 A35 2009
   759.4—dc22
   2009004287

                    10 9 8 7 6 5 4 3 2 1

Chronicle Books LLC
680 Second Street, San Francisco, California 94107
www.chroniclekids.com

www.metmuseum.org